What's the
Difference?

10 Animal Look-alikes

by Judy Diehl and David Plumb
illustrated by Vlasta van Kampen

Annick Press Ltd.
Toronto • New York • Vancouver

Introduction

Have you ever watched twins? At first they seem to be exactly alike, but when you look closer, small differences become apparent. One's nose is longer, the other has darker hair. Or, one has more freckles and the other is a little taller. The same applies in the animal world: there are many animals that, at first glance, appear to be alike, but on close examination are, indeed, quite different.

With animals that look similar, the differences are not always easy to see. And often there is not a simple set of rules to use in telling one animal from another. To make matters even more confusing, rules that apply to a certain animal in one country may not hold true for that same animal in another country! In fact, some of the animal pairs presented in these pictures would never be found together in the wild. In the illustrations they appear side-by-side in their natural habitats, for easy comparison.

What's the Difference looks at ten animal pairs that are easily confused. Within the text the authors have pointed out some of the main differences in appearance. This book is a great starting point for kids to learn how to look carefully at animals and the world they inhabit.

By learning more about the great diversity to be found in nature, the world truly becomes an amazing playground for the mind and imagination.

Contents

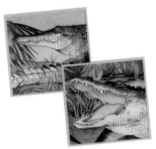

Leopards and cheetahs

Leopard

Cheetah

Sleek, spotted cats, running, pouncing on their prey. Do those spots belong to a leopard or a cheetah?

If you have trouble telling a cheetah from a leopard, you're not alone. Spotting the differences between these big spotted cats can be tricky.

Cheetahs are the fastest mammals in the world. A cheetah has long legs for chasing gazelles, zebras, and other quick-moving animals that it eats. Over short distances, a cheetah can race as fast as a car zooming down the highway. A leopard has shorter legs and can't run as quickly. It catches its prey by sneaking up behind another animal, then pouncing on it.

Cheetahs and leopards have different faces, too. A cheetah has dark stripes that run down both sides of its face, from its eyes to its upper lip. A leopard doesn't have these markings. Its face is broader and heavier.

Another way to tell a cheetah from a leopard is to see which big cat climbs trees. You'll never see a full-grown cheetah up a tree. Its claws, which cannot completely draw back (or retract), are not suited for tree-climbing. All leopards, on the other hand, have claws that retract. Most leopards spend lots of time in trees, eating, sleeping, or waiting to pounce on animals that walk on the ground below.

Some leopards, called panthers, have dark-colored skin with spots that can be seen only in bright sunlight. You'll never spot a cheetah that looks like that!

Tortoises and turtles

Desert tortoise

Basking on a log, sleeping in the sun, they hide in their shells when danger threatens. Tortoises and turtles, how do you tell them apart?

Both tortoises and turtles are reptiles, animals that have skin covered with scales. It's easy to tell tortoises and turtles from other reptiles—tortoises and turtles are the only reptiles that have shells. These shells contain and protect the animals' bodies. Both turtles and tortoises cannot ever leave their shells because their backbones are part of their hard outer coverings.

With so much in common, you might wonder just what the difference is between tortoises and turtles. The answer is that tortoises are a particular kind of turtle. Tortoises are related to turtles in the same way that toads are related to frogs. (For more on toads and frogs, see page 15.)

The main difference between tortoises and most other turtles has to do with where they live. Tortoises always live on land. To move around, a tortoise counts on its sturdy, elephant-like feet. *Most* turtles that are not tortoises spend at least part of the time in water.

If you compare the shells of tortoises and most other turtles, you will find another difference. Tortoises generally have heavier shells than turtles that go in water.

Eastern painted turtle

Wasps and bees

Honey bee

Common wasp

They have fast-beating wings and things that sting. Wasps and bees seem the same —but they're not!

Bees and wasps have a lot in common. They both belong to the same group of animals, called insects. Some bees and wasps (such as honeybees, bumblebees, and wasps called yellow jackets) even look alike, with black and yellow stripes.

But bees and wasps are also very different. Bees are covered in hair and look furrier than wasps. When bees walk over flowers, they use their hair to collect pollen and nectar. Back home, they feed the pollen to their young and sometimes use the nectar to make honey. Wasps don't gather pollen or nectar, so you won't see them around flowers as much as bees. Instead, they often hang out at picnics or around garbage cans where sweet things (like lemonade and ripe fruit) are found. Unlike bees, some wasps catch other insects, sting and paralyze them, then feed them to their young. Bees use their stingers to defend themselves, their homes, and their young from people and animals.

Both bumblebees and wasps have straight stingers that they pull out of their victims' bodies and use again and again. But honeybees can only sting once because they have a barbed stinger that stays stuck after it's been used. When a honeybee tries to fly away after stinging, it pulls out the part of its body attached to the stinger and dies. That never happens to a wasp!

Crocodiles and alligators

Crocodile

Alligator

Sleeping on the bank, dozing in the sun—splash! Watch out! A crocodile or an alligator, which is it?

Both alligators and crocodiles have long tails, short legs, sharp teeth, and scale-covered skin that looks like a suit of armor. These reptiles share similar looks, but they are also different.

One difference between wild alligators and crocodiles has to do with where they live. Alligators are found only in southeast United States and China. They generally live in or near fresh water (water found in lakes and rivers). Crocodiles, however, live in many parts of the world, including Africa, Asia, Australia, and North America. They live in or near salt water (water found in oceans and seas) as well as fresh water.

If you compare the crocodiles and alligators that are found in North America, you will spot other differences, too. American crocodiles have two bottom teeth that stick out when their mouths are closed. All American crocodiles show the same teeth—the fourth one from the front, on each side. American alligators don't have teeth that stick out when their jaws are shut.

The snouts of an American alligator and an American crocodile are different, too. An American alligator's snout is wider and rounder than the snout of an American crocodile. But don't expect to be able to tell all alligators and crocodiles apart by their snouts. Some crocodiles outside the United States have snouts that look more like an American alligator's snout!

Rabbits and hares

Rabbit

Hare (Jack Rabbit)

They have strong legs, long ears and short fluffy tails—rabbit or hare, how can you tell?

One of the best ways to tell a rabbit from a hare is to compare their babies. Newborn rabbits have pink, hairless skin and closed eyes. They are temporarily blind, very helpless, and rely on their mother, who doesn't leave them until their fur grows in. Baby hares, on the other hand, are born with full coats of fur and open eyes. Just a few minutes after they're born, hares are able to hop around. Their mother leaves them alone for long stretches of time, returning to feed them and care for them.

After rabbits and hares grow up, you can often notice other differences between them. Rabbits are usually smaller and lighter than hares. Hares have longer ears and legs, and run faster than rabbits.

However, comparing a wild rabbit's looks with a hare's looks isn't easy to do because these two mammals often live in different places. Rabbits prefer areas with lots of shrubs, plants, and trees. Many (but not all) rabbits dig burrows in the ground and live together with other rabbits in underground "towns" called warrens that are made of many connected burrows. Hares like to stay in open country, above ground. Instead of living in burrows, hares sleep, find shelter, and look after their young in shallow, hollowed-out spots in the ground called forms.

Toads and frogs

American toad

They croak and hop, they leap and swim. Are they toads or frogs?

Frogs are amphibians, animals with backbones that can live in water and on land. Frogs come in many sizes and colors and are found almost everywhere in the world. All together, there are more than 20 different groups, called families, of frogs.

And what about toads? Toads are the members of only one family of frogs. In other words, toads are a particular kind of frog. Toads are related to frogs in the same way that tortoises are related to turtles. (See page 7 for more on tortoises and turtles.)

In most parts of the world, however, it's much more difficult to tell what's a toad and what's not—unless you are a scientist who studies frogs. These amphibian experts examine the shape of a frog's bones and compare them with other frog bones in order to know for certain which family the frog belongs to. It's no wonder people sometimes get confused about what a tortoise is and what a turtle is. Even the words "tortoise" and "turtle" sound similar.

However, you can easily spot the differences between toads and other frogs in some parts of the world. England is one of those places. Only two frog families live there. Toads found in England are covered in warty skin, have short back legs used for hopping, and live on land. Other frogs in England are smooth-skinned, have long back legs for leaping, and live in the water.

Northern leopard frog

15

Ravens and crows

Raven

Big black birds—some sit in trees, others swoop and soar in the sky. Are they ravens or crows?

It might be easy to spot some of the differences between crows and ravens if you could see these two birds side by side. However, crows and ravens aren't usually found together—they often live in different places. Crows are found mostly in low-lying, flat places. Ravens, on the other hand, live in high mountains and also in northern regions where crows aren't usually found.

If you were able to see some crows and ravens together, you would notice differences in their size and appearance. Crows are smaller than ravens and have smooth feathers on their throats. Ravens have throat feathers that are shaggy and ruffled-looking. Crows and ravens have different beaks, too. A raven's beak is larger and more curved than the one a crow has. And when these birds open their beaks and call out, they make different sounds—crows caw, ravens croak.

There are other ways of telling crows apart from ravens. Crows often fly in flocks, while ravens tend to be alone. When crows fly, you can see their fan-shaped tails. Unlike crows, ravens have wedge-shaped tails. And crows can do something ravens can't do—a crow can leap off the ground straight into the air. A raven is so heavy that it often has to take two or three hops before it can take off.

Crow

Butterflies and moths

Tiger Swallowtail
butterfly

They flitter and flutter, they twirl and swirl—can you tell a butterfly from a moth?

Butterflies and moths are insects with something extra—they are covered with thousands of tiny colored scales, from the tip of their feelers all the way to their feet. The scales overlap, like shingles on a roof, and make the patterns you see on the wings of butterflies and moths.

Butterflies and moths are so closely related, and seem so similar, that it's easy to miss the differences between them. Most butterflies have feelers with knobs at the tips. Most moths have either plain, hair-like antennae or feathery feelers without knobs. Sometimes you can spot a butterfly by the way it holds its wings straight up while resting. Most moths don't do this. Instead, they rest with their wings flat, over their bodies.

The time of day when you see these insects might also tell you if you are looking at a butterfly or a moth. Most butterflies are active during the day and most moths are active at night. Butterflies tend to be brightly colored, while moths are not. However, some butterflies behave more like moths, and some moths seem to be like butterflies! That's why you can't always count on rules to tell butterflies and moths apart.

Prothea moth

Donkeys and mules

Mule

Donkey

Long legs running, big ears listening. Hee haw! That's not a horse; but, is it a donkey or a mule?

Like other animals that people have trouble telling apart, donkeys and mules are alike in some ways and different in other ways. Donkeys and mules are both related to horses. Donkeys and mules also share some similar physical features. They both have smaller hooves and larger ears than those of a horse of similar size. The noses, mouths, and jaws (or "muzzles") of donkeys are light in color. So are their bellies and legs. Mules often have light-colored muzzles and bellies, too.

But not everything about mules and donkeys is similar. If you compare a donkey's legs with the legs of a mule, you will spot some differences between them. A donkey has short legs in relation to its body. A mule has longer legs, more like a horse's legs. And, unlike a donkey, a mule usually has legs that are the same color as its body, not its belly.

There is also an important difference between female donkeys and female mules. Female donkeys, after mating with male donkeys, are able to give birth to baby donkeys. However, female mules cannot ever produce babies. Baby mules are born *only* to female horses that have mated with male donkeys. With a horse for a mother and a donkey for a father, it's no wonder a mule looks like a horse—with the ears of a donkey!

Porpoises and dolphins

Dall's porpoise

They jump, they splash, they swim and play. How do you tell a porpoise from a dolphin?

Dolphins and porpoises may look like fish, but they are actually whales, mammals that live in the water. Like all mammals, dolphins and porpoises breathe air and drink milk from their mother.

Some species of dolphins and some species of porpoises look so similar that it is difficult to find the differences between these two whales simply by looking at them and comparing them. This is true in most parts of the world, where many dolphins and porpoises live together. To tell a dolphin from a porpoise in those places, you must ask a whale expert for help. These scientists examine the animal's skull and teeth in order to know for certain whether it is a dolphin or a porpoise.

Europe, however, is one place where you can spot the differences between dolphins and porpoises. Only a few species of dolphins and one species of porpoise live there and there are noticeable differences between the dolphins and the porpoises. A porpoise that lives in European waters has teeth that look like spades (small shovels), a short triangle-shaped back fin, and small, almost oval flippers. A dolphin that lives in the same waters is larger and less tubby than a porpoise and has a "beak" that sticks out on its face. Its back fin is curved and its flippers are shaped like triangles.

Common dolphin

Special thanks to the *Canadian Museum of Nature* for scientific consultation.

To Goblin, Shadow and Blaze, the originals.
—J.D. and D.P.

For Joe and Leslie with love and affection.
—V.v.K.

We acknowledge the support of the Canada Council for the Arts, the Ontario Arts Council, and the Government of Canada through the Book Publishing Industry Development Program (BPIDP) for our publishing activities.

Cataloging in Publication Data

Diehl, Judy
    What's the difference?

ISBN 1-55037-565-2 (bound)   ISBN 1-55037-564-4 (pbk.)

1. Animals – Juvenile literature.   I. Plumb, David, 1959- .
II. van Kampen, Vlasta.   III. Title.

QL49.D53 2000   j590   C00-930428-2

The art in this book was rendered in watercolors.
The text was typeset in Cheltenham.

Distributed in Canada by: Published in the U.S.A. by Annick Press (U.S.) Ltd.
Firefly Books Ltd.   Distributed in the U.S.A. by:
3680 Victoria Park Avenue   Firefly Books (U.S.) Inc.
Willowdale, ON   P.O. Box 1338
M2H 3K1   Ellicott Station
    Buffalo, NY 14205

Printed and bound in Canada by Friesens, Altona, Manitoba.

Visit us at: www.annickpress.com

GLOSSARY

Amphibians

Amphibians are animals with backbones that may live both on land and in water. Amphibians depend on the temperature of their surroundings for warming up or cooling down their bodies. Some people refer to this as "cold-blooded," but amphibians are only truly cold-blooded when their surroundings are cold. All amphibians have moist skin, and none have hair, scales, or feathers.

Reptiles

Like amphibians, reptiles are animals with backbones that may live both on land and in water. Reptiles have well-armored skins that are usually completely covered by scales. Their skin helps them to avoid losing too much water, so they can live in dry places. Reptiles depend on the temperature of their surroundings for warming up or cooling down their bodies. Some people refer to this as "cold-blooded," but reptiles are only truly cold-blooded when their surroundings are cold.

Insects

Insects are animals without backbones that have bodies divided into three parts, three pairs of legs, one pair of feelers (or antennae), and, usually, one or two pairs of wings. Insects have skeletons that are on the outside of their bodies.

Birds

Birds are animals that have backbones, bodies covered in feathers, and wings. All birds lay hard-shelled eggs. Some scientists believe that birds and some kinds of dinosaurs—ancient reptiles—shared a common ancestor that existed many millions of years ago. For this reason, birds are now sometimes grouped together with reptiles.

Mammals

Mammals are animals with backbones that breathe air, are usually covered in hair, and drink milk from their mothers. Adult mammals can control their own body temperature – they do not depend on the temperature of their surroundings for warming up or cooling down their bodies.